Quick Guide II: How to Spot, Mimic and Become a Top Salesperson

For new or seasoned sales professionals, managers and CEOs

Number 2 in a series of articles by

Paul C Burr PhD

http://paulcburr.com/

Acknowledgements

Romilla Ready, Lead Author, Neuro-linguistic Programming for Dummies®

Penelope Walsh, Book Reviewer

Contents

Summary Bullet Points

This 17-page article (A4 size, excluding appendices) bears from my research, consulting, direct selling and coaching within global corporations over a twenty year period. The companies I worked directly for, or in a freelance capacity with, include: IBM, Cisco, Accenture, Xerox, American Express, Standard Chartered, BP and Reckitt Benckiser. During this period I've had the privilege to meet and work with hundreds of top performers worldwide.

Within you will discover how and why top salespeople succeed through:

• Effectiveness = motivation x confidence x competence x curiosity (or $E=MC^3$)

• Migrating from selling at D-Level (middle management) to C-Level (senior management) involves a journey, from a tangible and known environment to one of uncertainty and the unknown

• Engaging a customer effectively and willingly, to co-explore uncertainty and the unknown, requires a salesperson to demonstrate *7 key traits*, characteristics and competencies

1. *Faith-in-self*
2. *Curiosity*
3. *Composure*
4. *Sensibility*
5. *Co-opting*
6. *Inspirational*
7. *Passion*

• Top salespeople demonstrate that:

- The aforementioned *7 key traits* are what really differentiate top performers from 'moderates', more so than behaviours in that they predict whether the salesperson will be successful selling directly to C-level clients.

- You can spot a top-performer or high-potential individual by noticing how much they demonstrate these *7 key traits*.

- These key traits are nurtured not 'trained in the classroom'; the nurturing process can be accelerated by equipping yourself with 'non-expert' coaching tools, such as in *Appendix 2 - Prepare to Be at your Peak in Every Meeting.*

Top Selling Is about the 'How' as well as the 'What'

Over and above exemplary sales achievements, how do 'you' (by 'you' I mean: you, me, us, we) spot a top salesperson when you meet one? If you want to sell as well as they do or be just like them, how would you go about it? If you were to ask the same questions and give the same answers as they do, would that be enough?

No, because you bring your own personality and mannerisms into the equation. 'Acting as if' helps pave the way but there's something about how top salespeople come across to customers. It requires the wisdom and will to mimic how they sell as well as the sales process they follow (the 'what they do differently' - see *Quick Guide: How Top Salespeople Sell*). In fact, if you really do want to become and stay a top salesperson, it's vital!

To mimic the 'how', you'll need to assimilate what goes on below the surface of top salespeople's personae, their distinguishing traits and characteristics; the mannerisms with which they approach selling. Before we go into detail, let's note the changes in context that salespeople deal with as they migrate from selling from middle managers (D-level) to senior managers (C-level) clients.

As they progress through their career, successful salespeople find themselves selling higher value solutions to higher level clients. Value and risk often go hand in hand; the higher the value of a sale, the bigger the risk involved.

At some level, risk is the emotional anxiety (fear) we attach to things not turning out the way we want. The more the risk, the higher the propensity for fear, uncertainty and doubt to emerge in the minds of stakeholders involved. The more risk involved in a proposition, the more trust we need to put in suppliers to compensate.

Trust is the gap between what we know and what we put faith in.

The customers' generic questions about trust and value (see *Quick Guide: How Top Salespeople Sell*) remain the same. It is what goes on below the surface of the selling-buying dialogue that can shift. Top salespeople stay attuned to these shifts, especially shifts in the customers' passions and fears.

Being aware of fear, staying attuned comes from knowing what questions to ask, how to ask them and when to ask them. You could say it's a skill or competency developed over time. It also requires more than the intellectual process of knowing what and how to ask (and respond to) questions. It requires faith-in-self, composure and genuine curiosity to ask questions about fear, uncertainty and doubt - so that you don't...

• Project your unwarranted fear, uncertainty and doubt on to the customer

or

• Come across as asking rhetorical questions to make the customer feel as if you're trying to control the dialogue.

I remember a sales campaign, for a large management consulting intervention, by a client of mine. The salesperson had manipulated a conversation so that his customer revealed all their shortcomings. He wanted the customer to see how much they needed his company's services. The customer became irritated and subsequently spent over a million pounds with another independent consulting firm to 'review all the exposures' that the salesperson had brought to their attention.

Later, my coaching sessions helped the salesperson realise that he had reflected his own fears as much as point out those of the customer. With benefit of hindsight and insight, his 'do differently' would have been to explore the issues with the customer, one issue at a time; not try to control a conversation that purposefully left the customer in a void. I reminded him of a sales maxim derived from ancient wisdom...

If you want to change a customer's perspective stop trying to control it.

The aforementioned maxim requires a large amount of faith, faith-in-self. It also implies a large amount of sensibility, as to where the customer is at in their frame of mind.

Like a skill or competency, a trait or characteristic is something you demonstrate to customers. Unlike a skill or competency, a trait or characteristic is not typically something you pick up in a class room and improve through experience. Instead, you nurture it. For example, as mentioned prior, faith-in-self and sensibility: two of *7 key traits* I've observed top salespeople demonstrate more than 'moderates'.

'Nurturing' a trait, I suggest, is the domain of 'non-expert' coaching where sales managers (or external coaches, like me) can step in. Many sales managers I meet make good sales mentors. Few practice 'coaching', i.e. the nurturing of winning traits and characteristics.

(For further explanation of the role of a sales manager as a 'non-expert' coach - which differs from that of a 'sales mentor' - see *Appendix 3.*)

———

Effectiveness = Motivation x Confidence x Competence x Curiosity (*$E{=}MC^3$*)

Most sales training I've come across focuses primarily on developing a salesperson's skills or competencies, for example: opening, qualifying, questioning, advocating, presenting, negotiating and closing. The intention is that, over time with experience, the salesperson will get better and better at demonstrating these skills. It follows logically that they'll become more confident in their sales approach and thus hopefully more motivated.

I haven't seen much in the way of material that focuses on engendering an ongoing sense of curiosity, for example, how can I be the best, if not better, at what I sell?

The $E{=}MC^3$ equation implies that an individual's effectiveness is three parts mental and emotional (motivation, competence and curiosity) to one part intellectual (competence).

Let's take a first pass at each of the qualities: motivation, confidence, competence and curiosity. We'll return to some specifics in chapter, *7 Key Traits of a Top Salesperson*.

Motivation

Most salespeople are motivated to win, especially when the selling is relatively easy. Likewise most are motivated by earnings and win bonuses. Some are motivated by advancing their career.

What motivates top salespeople? The answers from my research fall into three categories:

1. *"To be the best I can be"* or *"...recognised as the best salesperson there is"* - not only the best in terms of results but the best at selling too (outcomes + journey).

2. *"To deliver customer value above and beyond that expected."*

3. *"To create a legacy so that I am renowned for the value I bring to customers and my organisation's business."*

In all three categories, the top performers are motivated by being (and being seen as) excellent. 'Moderates' talk of winning and earnings but talk less of personal excellence.

Confidence

I worked with a 26 year old CEO of a recruitment firm who had a good reputation for hiring confident as opposed to arrogant people. I was asked to model how he went about the task. Our conversation went something like this:

Me: *"How do you differentiate between a confident person and an arrogant one?"*

CEO: *"Well, I'm not sure; I just get a 'feeling'."*

Me: *"Describe that 'feeling'."*

CEO: *"Well you just sort of know, don't you? It's something you sense..... a gut feeling."*

Me: *"Okay, imagine you have an arrogant person to your left and a confident to your right. What's the difference between them?"*

CEO: *"The confident person asks questions; the arrogant person doesn't. The confident person probes for where they feel they'll bring value to the organisation. They look to find out if they will enjoy the role. They seek opportunities for themselves to grow in the role. The arrogant person takes a position that they have the knowledge and wisdom suitable for the job and makes no effort to see how well they'll fit in."*

Top salespeople exude confidence by the quality of questions they ask as well as the articulacy by which they convey reassurance. (For a framework with which to construct quality sales questions, refer to the INCREASE™ model in Number 1 of this series of business articles, *Quick Guide - How Top Salespeople Sell.*)

Competence

If you stacked all the sales training and development materials in the world on top of one another, you'd probably build a mountain higher than Mount Everest. So I'll attempt to put a different slant on competence by giving you a customer's perspective. (For completeness, Appendix 1 lists the skills and knowledge demonstrated by top salespeople at, and away from, the customer interface.)

A corporate salesperson spends, on average, 15% of their time speaking directly to a customer. Ergo, 85% of the time, they apply their skills and knowledge to researching, developing and planning; how to be more effective during the '15%' customer interface window when the occasion arises.

Top performers prepare themselves, intellectually and psychologically, to be at their peak when speaking to the customer. They develop appropriate skills and knowledge (the intellectual exchange) and they also prepare themselves to be in the right frame of mind and body (the mental and emotional exchange) with the customer.

Being perceived as 'competent' by the customer requires you to be:

1. Prepared: with insightful questions to ask and have answers to potential customer questions, including facts, data and logic so that your proposals are both visionary, 'grounded in reality' and hopefully compelling

2. Clear about the outcomes: What do you want to achieve in the meeting both in terms of the task-in-hand and your relationship with the customer (e.g. engender trust). It's also being very clear about the outcomes the customer might want to achieve, in terms of their task-in-hand and from their relationship with a supplier like you.

Illustration: 4 Outcomes to a Meeting

	You	Customer
Task in hand	1	3
Change to relationship	2	4

Most of us prepare 'box 1' before a meeting. Many 'moderates' omit boxes 2 and 3 above from their preparatory work. Most salespeople miss out box 4 altogether - often because of a lack of self-belief and sometimes unconsciously. They don't visualise themselves in a picture working closely with the customer.

3. In the right frame of mind: If you were to prioritise the three factors: Prepared, Clear Outcomes and Frame of Mind - which order would you place them?

Exercise: Allocate three weighting percentages (that add up to 100%) against Prepared, Clear Outcomes and Frame of Mind respectively - in terms of how important they are to being successful during (not before) a meeting.

Research shows...

The most important thing you take into a meeting is your frame of mind.

This statement often raises a few queries. It doesn't say that you shouldn't prepare diligently for a meeting. What it says instead is - the moment the meeting starts, the single most important factor that will determine your success is your frame of mind. You may well feel you have to do a significant amount of preparation to get yourself 'centred', for example. BUT it's not the process the meeting follows that determines success the most; it's you, your frame of mind and the thoughts that engender that frame of mind.

Specifically, whatever thought you process in your conscious mind passes straight into your unconscious mind and merges with any 'subconscious programmes' running there. The aggregate information is then passed directly to your DNA which vibrates at different rates in accord with your temperament. That is:

The vibe you put out determines your success.

I coached a very successful salesperson who never felt at her best in front of a CEO customer. It took a wee while for us to discover a subconscious programme she'd developed from her authoritarian parents, created by a 'single significant emotional event' when she was three years old. Once she 'released' this programme, her faith-in-self in front of CEO's increased significantly. Her sales soared.

Research by scientists (e.g. *The Biology of Belief*, by Dr Bruce Lipton and *The Genie in your Genes*, by Dr Matthew Dawson) demonstrates the subliminal communicative functioning power of DNA between human beings which can be harmonious (I prefer the term, 'resonant') or out of tune (dissonant) - and at its extreme, disruptive.

Allow me to define 'being competent' as not only having the capability to demonstrate requisite skills and knowledge at the customer interface, it's also about being competent at preparing yourself to be at your peak (see *Appendix 2*), to achieve the gravitas (sometimes called 'traction') you seek.

Author's note: gravitas is something we can all achieve; it's a result not a gift privy to a chosen few. Only 15% or so of salespeople achieve the 'customer gravitas' they seek, hence this book!

Let me add, the competence that customers attribute to you will also include an element of the perceived competence of the solutions you bring to the table, i.e. an acknowledgement of the potential of your solution's value proposition. Put another way, if the customer has little faith in what you're selling, even though they value your personal contribution, to what degree will you be invited to participate in the decision making process?

We've covered two of the three *'Cs'* in the *E=MC³* equation. A salesperson not only has to be competent in following 'top sales processes' (and have potentially 'competent' solutions); they need to be confident in their ability and motivated to follow those sales processes too. And still there's one further factor that determines how effective you are (by seeing what's really going on), a heightened sense of...

Curiosity

Top salespeople are unstintingly curious. For example, they love to be coached. They are very willing to learn how to become more effective at selling.

Top performers focus on working smarter, not harder, than 'moderates'

You might ask, *"Curious about what?"* Answer: *"Everything!"*

Top salespeople probe below the surface of what's going on - especially when forging business relationships. Like a metaphorical iceberg, they acknowledge that you only see about 15% above the surface; the obvious facts and logic by which a customer makes a decision. But they don't stop there, they're proactive to find the real passions and fears which will motivate or deter key stakeholders in the decision making process.

Curiosity is the sonar signal you emit to track changes on your 'sales radar screen'. You track political, economic, sociological, technological and organisational developments as well as your competitors' manoeuvres. At the deepest level, you're tuning into changes in customers' feelings, e.g. inspiration, motivation, confidence, sense of security, anger and most of all - trust and fear.

There's more. You also need to be proactively curious about what might happen. I return to this later.

To summarise: selling is three parts mental/emotional to one part intellectual.

$E=MC^3$, it's not rocket science!

Self Assessment and Coaching Tips: How to Improve your Effectiveness...

Give yourself a score out of 10 for how motivated you really feel right now (10 = perfect, 5 = average, 0 = nowhere). Repeat the process three times, giving yourself scores out of 10 for your levels of confidence, competence and curiosity respectively.

If you've given yourself a minimum score of 7 for each category (7x7x7x7 = 2,401 out of 10,000 maximum) then you are in the zone of being or becoming a top performer.

Note: there's plenty of headroom to between 2,401 and 10,000 to become 'perfect'. There's plenty of scope by which you can improve your effectiveness. And, without hopefully spoiling your anticipation, as you approach a series of 10s, your definition of 'perfect' enhances. Up high, you can see more clearly and farther into the distance. You give yourself a choice to 'land at 10' or 'refuel in flight' to go beyond.

If you have any scores less than a '7', raise those scores to at least a 7 to begin with.

If all your scores are 7 or more then focus on raising your curiosity and you'll find that the others will follow.

If, for example, you don't feel very curious, 'act-as if!' Find yourself or think of a role model of someone whom you know to be very curious. Pretend 'that they are you; that you are them'. Do what they might do to nurture the feeling (vibration) of curiosity in your body's 'muscle memory'.

From 'Selling Solutions' to 'Selling Directions'

The better you sell, the bigger the sales targets you're given. Higher sales, when achieved through higher value propositions to customers, means 'higher calling'. As you start calling higher in a customer organisation's hierarchy, above say the level of a business unit manager, you step into the unknown.

Up to 'business unit level', you find people, by and large, whose job is replicated elsewhere in their organisation, with the same types of budgets and targets to achieve. There's plenty of repetition and thus there are plenty of experts or 'knowledge managers' in organisational processes. Up to this level, the business unit environment is considered tangible, measurable and thus manageable.

Above this level you begin to meet people whose job involves changing their company. By definition, 'change' means doing things differently to achieve different results.

Illustration: The Executive's Journey - Create Tomorrow's Reality

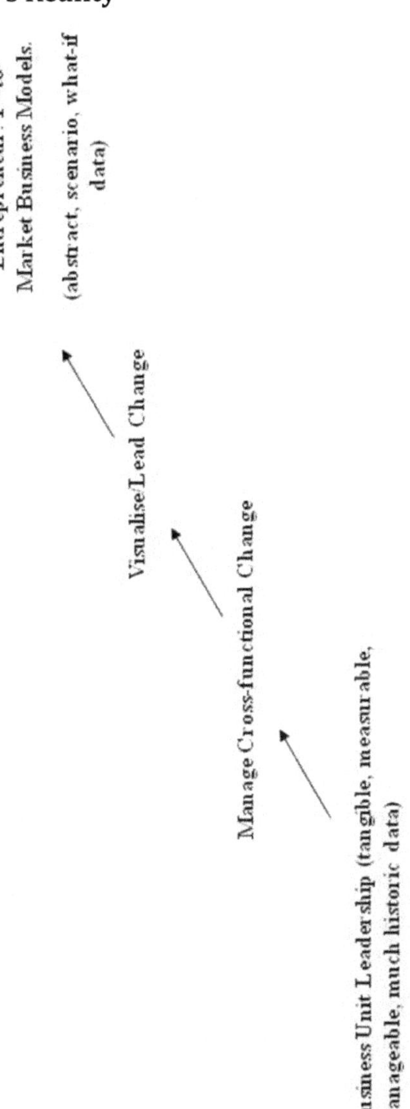

When you do something for the first time, you can't guarantee you'll get the results you want first time. (So it's about having the composure, curiosity and faith-in-self to learn quickly from unwanted outcomes.) Ergo, there's an element of the unknown to work with.

As you call higher in the organisation, you meet people who are the leaders and visionaries of change, broader-based change. They deal with more unknowns and uncertainty.

As you call higher still, you meet those who attempt to build '1st-to-market' products and business services, often from a number of scenarios and 'what-if-questions'. They study the big if not global picture - the interactions between the political, economic, sociological and technological futures. (For example, the lines between the retail and banking sectors have all but dissipated in recent years.) Once upon a time, CEOs and strategists used to study years into the future. With the ever increasing rapidity of change in technology, they now study medium (sometimes short) term futures with increasing levels of the unknown and uncertainty.

The future happens a lot sooner these days.

As a salesperson starts to ascend the customer's hierarchy of management, they must learn to equip themselves for the climb - to match the specific needs and expectations of senior customers. They must adjust as well to the environment those senior customers operate in.

The stakes are much 'higher'!

Top salespeople journey from...

• An environment where they are selling to 'experts' with today's tangible, measurable and manageable problems and opportunities

To...

• A level in the organisation where people are 'explorers', 'direction setters', 'thought leaders' and '1st to market entrepreneurs'; focusing on opportunities with the most unknowns, uncertainties and potential doubts.

The salesperson's journey requires them to earn the right to become a trusted, fellow 'explorer' and 'map reader' whilst retaining the elements of expertise in their own industry to bring to the planning table.

They need to switch from being reactive to more and more proactive, so that they are 'surfing the wave into the unknown' alongside, if not slightly ahead of, the customer. They become a 'valued scout'.

They migrate from selling products, to solutions, to participating in the direction setting of their customer's organisation.

Ideally, they become privy to the customers' fears that come from dealing with the ambiguity and unknowns of a corporation's future.

You can count the number of world-class 'industry experts' who sell into vast corporations on the fingers of one hand. Emulating them is not what this article is about.

Illustration: From Selling Products/Services to Solutions, to Directions - the Quantum Shift

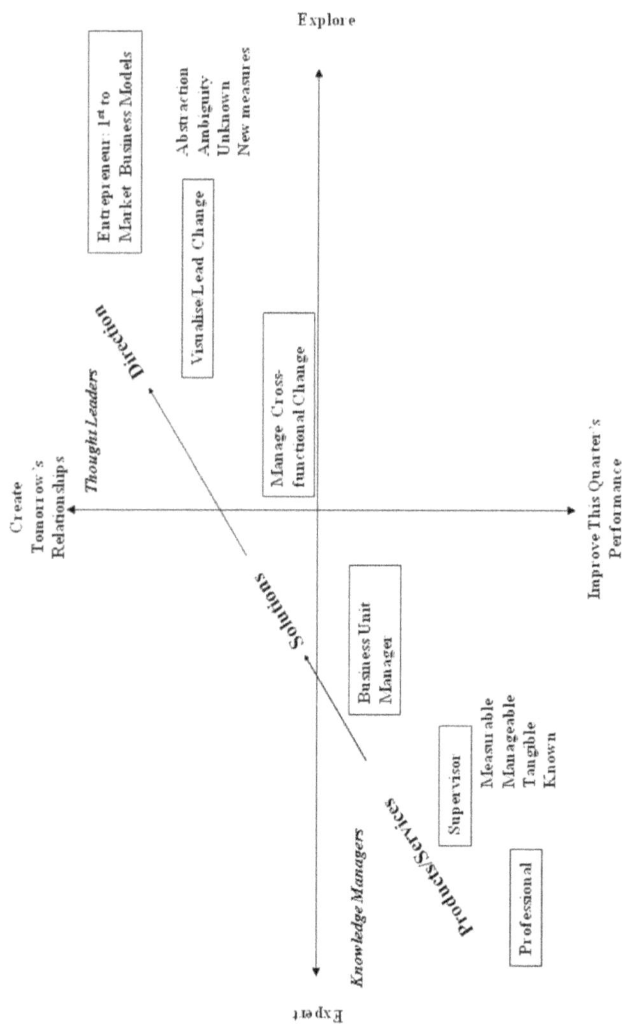

It's about what it takes for a salesperson to succeed in making the *switch*:

• From products, services and solutions that deal with today's problems and opportunities - to 'selling a direction' for the future?

• From a known, tangible, measurable and manageable customer environment - to an environment that deals with abstraction, unknowns, uncertainties and thus the potential for fears and doubts (that are often not verbalised without probing for them).

Over years of research, I detected and isolated *7 key traits* by which you can predict if a salesperson is suitably equipped to make the *switch*. These traits didn't appear overnight. I started off by studying two of the seven. As the number of traits grew, some of their definitions remained a little blurred around the edges. As my understanding grew, the terms I use and their descriptions have evolved too. For example, what started as self-trust, I now use the term, faith-in-self, which embraces self-trust (explained in next chapter).

The list that follows is thus a 'living agenda' and open to improvement. I'm not claiming it's complete. It represents work in progress and the best picture, I know of, with which to profile a top salesperson.

---

7 Key Traits of a Top Salesperson

This does not say that top salespeople don't have other traits in common with moderate performers. Instead, this chapter isolates the traits which top salespeople demonstrate significantly more than 'moderates'. There's a 'synergistic chemistry' between these traits too. The traits feed one another. Their combined effect is greater than the sum of the individual parts.

In all seven traits, you'll observe a 'matching' of the characteristics that leaders of change in customer organisations are developing, in order to succeed if not survive. There is a simple test to check the validity of each of these traits as you read through them. Ask yourself, *"What would be the implications if a salesperson or business leader did not demonstrate this trait as part of their repertoire?"*

Recap: Traits are mostly nurtured, not trained. They signify the manner of how you sell rather than the sales process you follow.

1. Faith-in-Self

According to some historians, the secret of Julius Caesar's success was his timing, speed and responsiveness in the face of adversity with only the facts and data available in the moment.

Data mining and warehousing techniques facilitate the capacity to process vast amounts of data. By definition, they project a future, a continuum, based upon past trends. These days we encounter more and more rapid discontinuity. For example, the tragic self immolation of a Tunisian fruit seller, in protest of being denied his right to make a living, allegedly set off a chain of protests that within two months led to the Arab Spring. Any forecasts based on the cost of oil from a stable Middle-East Region went out the window. We observe more examples of highly improbable if not unthinkable events (Author, Nassim Nicholas Taleb, uses the phrase, *Black Swan* to describe such 'unseen-before' events).

Closer to USA and European corporate minds, can anyone predict accurately if, when and how the world's spiralling debt-based economy will turn around? I perhaps labour the point to exemplify the importance of self-trust. By self-trust, I encompass self-belief and confidence in the meaning.

Trust is the gap between what you know for fact and what you have faith in. You demonstrate faith-in-self by summoning the willpower and commitment (to self, principally) to put that self trust into action.

Willpower + commitment + self trust = faith-in-self

And...

If you don't demonstrate faith in yourself, how can you expect a customer to have faith in you?

Ultimately, faith-in-self is about living, being and selling truth, to the best of your consciousness knowledge. Truth drives out all falsity.

2. Curiosity

Curiosity combined with a strong faith-in-self triggers the salesperson to delve into the unknown; to seek and drive out all hidden falsity from their business relationships. If you have the best solution and your task of selling was purely intellectual then selling would be a 'breeze', would it not?

At the highest level, the salesperson's task is to understand the hidden aspirations and fears that customer's don't talk about. To unearth this 'hidden information', customers would need to trust you (i.e.

your integrity and capability) to put it to good use. So we start to see how faith-in-self can attract faith in you by others. And your curiosity attracts the curiosity of others to find out how you can help them.

Furthermore, we start to see the emergent role of a salesperson as a coach, equipped with 'curiosity tools', to collaborate with the customer to explore future unknowns.

3. Composure

The bigger a sales bid, the more unknowns it brings. The more uncertainty, the more trust you need to earn, to bridge the gap between what the customer is certain about (known) and needs to believe in (unknown) - to make a decision in any supplier's favour.

I remember working with a global IT firm in which members of a neighbouring sales team were reaching the climax of a huge, multimillion dollar, long and drawn out sales campaign. In the days running up to the point the customer's decision was about to be made, I recall sales and sales support individuals being physically sick when they came into work.

They'd done the best they could but their 'unhealthy attachment' to winning the bid became obvious to the customer. Their nervousness spread to the customer. The customer's trust in their ability, to resolve one last major issue, waned. Although favoured to win, they lost the bid during the last week of the campaign.

Top salespeople detach themselves from winning but not the passion for the journey of winning.

There is a difference. As they get closer to a big deal, top salespeople keep asking, *"What further information does the customer require to make a decision?"* And here's maybe a surprising thing, even if that information might mean that the customer will choose another supplier. They have the faith-in-self to provide what the customer needs.

They know that you can win a single sale based on an untruth, or shall we say a 'semi-truth'. But if, as and when the customer finds you out, all trust 'flies out the window'.

Furthermore, top salespeople don't take setbacks too personally. They remain composed whether they're winning or losing, accepted or rebuffed.

I interviewed a salesperson who excelled at cold calling. I went through his approach and how he prepared himself to perform what to many people, including me, is an onerous task. It was when I asked the following question, he gave me his 'golden nuggets to successful cold calling'...

Q: *"As you think about the whole process of cold calling, what's important to you?"*

A: *"The most important thing to get right about cold calling is my mindset. I have two beliefs:*

1. The customer who can make the best use of the service I offer is the least likely to be willing to say 'yes' to a request for an appointment. They are, by and large, 'time paupers'.

2. Their saying 'no' is a reflection of their busy-ness. It's not about me or my product's capability. They are not saying 'no' to me; they are saying 'no' to the outside world that might offer them help.

So I ask them, 'Is that no, you're not interested in what I have to offer. Or is it no, you do not have time right now. And if indeed that is the case, is there a time in the future that you feel it will be okay for me to contact you again?'

More often than not they will give me a time to call them back, say six weeks later. When I call them, I refer to the time and date of our original conversation. You'd be surprised how that little attention to detail seems to get their interest so that they are willing to give me time for an exploratory call."

4. Sensibility

When you feel sorry for someone you sympathise. When you share your understanding of another's feelings you empathise. My definition of sensibility goes beyond empathy; to describe an awareness and responsiveness to the intellectual (logic) as well as the mental and emotional position a client takes. Top salespeople have a profound ability to stand in the client's shoes to the extent that they can say to themselves, *"If I were the client, I would take the exact same actions as they are taking".* This is not sympathy or empathy, it is awareness of how, where and why the customer sees things differently to the salesperson. (After all, if they had the exact same views as you, you wouldn't need to do any selling.)

Business text books, I've come across, reason that two people have different perspectives about something because they followed different logic to get where they are, or they started from a different place. But differences of opinion go beyond the intellectual.

They will have differing levels of fear - especially about the unknown. They will both possess subconscious counter intentions [ergo, they can't articulate what holds them back). They will have different preferences (e.g. big picture or attention to detail; achievement before people or vice-versa; a scientific (facts, logic reason) or intuitive ('gut feel') approach].

Sensibility is the 'sense + ability' to stand in the client's shoes and use the appropriate logic and language patterns they prefer; thereby making a connection at intellectual, mental and emotional levels.

5. Co-opting

In a corporate environment it's a lot easier for the most successful salespeople to co-opt sales support resources. They have a reputation for winning and naturally, if you were in sales support you'd probably want to work on the projects that are most likely to succeed.

Top salespeople don't stop there. They have a relentless penchant for networking; calling high and wide in their own, customer and sometimes competitors' organisations, perhaps in offices that 'moderates' fear to tread.

Two Case Examples:

1. *"I look for 'movers and shakers' who have been successful in bringing about change in the customer's organisation - especially 'customer change' - and with whom, ideally, my competitors haven't yet formed a relationship.*

I call them and say 'I'm your sales representative from <ABC-Company> (a household name), I understand that you ran the <customer change> project. May I take 30 minutes of your time because if I don't I'm not doing my *job properly?'"* - A top salesperson in Egypt, who never achieved less than 1000% (one thousand) of their sales target, for ten consecutive years

2. I was coaching a CEO of a medium sized training company who was shortlisted along with one other company to provide a nationwide corporate training programme. Her company had the best training content and the competitor had a large network of competent trainers. The buying organisation used these factors to play the vendors off one another, to whittle down the price. Neither vendor had a compelling and economically viable solution in isolation of one another.

The CEO and I were using an imagery technique to foster creative action. She came up with the image of a 'wise panther'. I asked the question, *"So what would a 'wise-panther' do?"*

The next day, my client made a 200 mile journey to visit the CEO of the competitor. Within two hours she co-opted the competitor to approach the buyer with a combined and compelling bid. Everyone ended up a winner.

6. Inspirational

I interviewed a top salesperson in the UK Company of a Global-Top-5 IT organisation. I asked how he went about inspiring customer executives to take action.

He replied, *"Paul, this company is full of highly intelligent and clever people who know our technology inside out. But very few know how to articulate its value, as an integral part of a complex corporate proposition, in a compelling way, to the customer.*

And when you're selling at board level it's about taking the customer on a fantastic journey that's believable. That is, no matter how complex that journey is..., it's about breaking it down into manageable chunks. You create a pathway into the future that is as clearly marked out as possible. There will be uncharted territory. So it's about discerning all the parts of the map that are known from those unknown. It's then about pinpointing all the 'dots on the chart of the unknown'. That is, answering all the 'what if this happens' questions. In effect, you join the dots of the unknown with the customer as best you can."

Inspiration is the art of simplifying complexity and exploring uncertainty; to map out a journey with a destiny that the customer feels compelled to reach with you by their side.

7. Passion

Top salespeople have a passion for customer value. They see selling as a stepping stone enroute to the customer's as well as their own success.

Passion energises the life-force of selling. Top salespeople have a passion for selling, the journey to victory. They know that if they attach themselves to the winning and not the journey then they might lose their focus. They might start to make decisions borne out of fear. The results of which engender fear in others.

They know that the opposite of truth is not lies, it is fear. When a customer perceives fear, even subliminally, they detect that truth is being hidden from them. And so a lack of trust creeps into the relationship.

Top salespeople thus do not deny fear. For you cannot conquer what you do not recognise. Nor do they embrace fear; otherwise they would restrict themselves to the path (of not faith-in-trust) well trodden by 'moderates'. Instead they accept fear. They neither feed nor fight it. They simply let fear be. And fear acts like a child spoiling for attention. When it recognises that attention is not forthcoming, it eventually gets bored and will leave you alone.

There's a deeper level of learning here. Top salespeople don't try to conquer or control their fear. Instead, they learn how to allow fear to be and they learn to release it. They transform from being a 'brave warrior' into a 'magician'.

Brave warriors are fearless, magicians possess fearlessness; they know that their fears, no matter how much they perceive them to be real, are illusory and that by letting them be, eventually they leave. The top salesperson remains inwardly composed, which in turn directs their passion to focus on the path to victory, as well as the victory itself.

This is metaphorically akin to the way of the master in martial arts. The passion is for the perfect delivery of the blow that defeats the opponent as well as the victory.

There's a wonderful story about Bruce Lee, the legendary martial arts master. He became famous by beating other martial arts masters whose repertoire consisted of thousands of moves. Lee, by comparison, used relatively few moves but he practiced each technique a thousand times every day. His passion for perfection paved the path to his success.

Top salespeople have a passion to be recognised as the best - not only the best in terms of results (achievements) but also the best at selling (the path). More than this, they are driven by self recognition - that they've followed and lived a passion for truth, perfection.

The Law of Business Attraction

The aggregate of how well you demonstrate the aforementioned *7 key traits* informs the 'vibe' that you put out to customers and those around you. That vibe determines what you attract and who you inspire.

Recap: your mannerisms and intentions influence the thoughts in your conscious mind. What happens in your conscious mind passes to your unconscious mind and merges with the subconscious intentions and counter intentions held there i.e. hidden drives and anxieties that, by definition, you hold but are unaware of. (You can start to see how coaching to release subconscious counter intentions can dramatically improve your effectiveness.)

The unconscious mind directly influences the vibration that your DNA projects outwards. And that signal attracts and amplifies like-for-like traits and characteristics in those around you.

I coached an experienced salesperson whose sales had fallen sharply. It was easy to blame the economy. Everyone's sales were down. But...

Like all conscientious salespeople, he worked extra hard. He made as many calls as he could. He 'crossed all the t's and dotted all the i's' in his call reports; to demonstrate his commitment and loyalty to his bosses.

When I asked what was driving him, his response was, *"Well I'm behind in my numbers and I want to catch up. I don't want to lose my job!"*

"So fear drives your actions?"

"Yeh, I've got a wife and kids to support", came the answer.

I then asked a series of questions:

Q: *"To what extent are your friends and colleagues sharing your fear?"*

A: *"Quite a few, it's at times like this that you find out who your friends are."*

Q: *"To what extent are your existing customers showing fear?"*

A: *"A few have intimated that I'm trying too hard and come across as more pushy than usual. They are a bit apprehensive about me."*

Q: *"And what of new customers and prospects?"*

A: *"Again, everybody I meet seems fearful to do anything right now, even when the business case is clear cut."*

The coaching thus focused on helping the salesperson to release his fears. Guess what? Within a few weeks his sales started to go up and by the end of the coaching programme he flourished with a renewed sense of 'fearlessness'.

———

Self Assessment and Coaching Tips: Measure How 'Perfect' You Are...

Perform a similar exercise to that cited earlier. Give yourself a score out of 10 for how well you feel you demonstrate each of the 7 key traits. Focus on getting every score up to at least a 7, first of all.

You can ask other people to give you a score according to their perceptions of how they see you in action. Choose people whose views you value but don't necessarily see eye to eye with. You might get a more robust answer.

Truth drives out falsity in relationships. That falsity is borne of fear. When that fear is released, you allow truth to flow between you and your customer.

At the end of your career what do you want to look back on, a life filled with truth or decisions and manipulations borne out of fear? I have done both and hopefully far less of the latter in recent times.

As the Bard said...

This above all: to thine ownself be true,

And it must follow, as the night the day,

Thou canst not then be false to any man.

Farewell: my blessing season this in thee!

Lord Polonius in Hamlet, Act 1, Scene III.

(End of main body of article)

Thank you...

I plan to write further business articles (each 10-15 A4 pages) in this *Quick Guide* series. The next has the working title, *Quick Guide III: The Pillars of Successful Business Relationships.*

If you'd like further information about the variety of services I engage in, please visit these websites:

http://paulcburr.com/ ~ extensive and ethereal blog-site that combines business and ancient wisdom

http://www.facebook.com/PaulCBurr ~ over 15,000 followers

http://twitter.com/paulburr

www.cotoco.com ~ for 'wisdom- transfer' solutions; to pass on what the top performers in your organisation do differently from the 'moderates'.

or mailto: *doctapaul@paulcburr.com*

Appendix 1: Corporate Sales Competencies

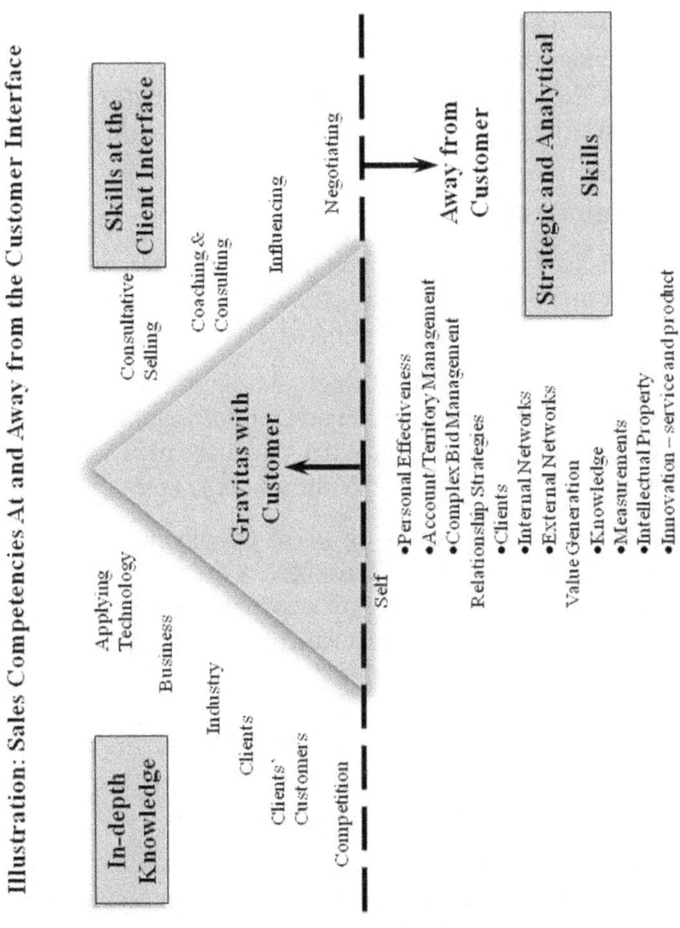

Gravitas with the Customer

To hold some level of customer gravitas with the customer, they will expect you to demonstrate both knowledge and skills. With gravitas you achieve a higher degree of 'customer intimacy', i.e. you know (because they share) their innermost aspirations and fears. When you know, and your competitors don't know; the customer is entrusting you with a unique opportunity to help them.

1. Knowledge

In no particular order, you'll need to meet or surpass customers' expectations of how knowledgeable they want you, their salesperson, to be:

- **Competition:** everything and anything about the organisations and people you compete against. Most of all you need to find out what the customers value and don't value about their offerings versus yours.

- **Client:** is about knowing all the people involved in the client's decision making process, especially those who have the power of veto over what you're seeking to achieve with the client. Specifically, you'll want to know their disposition (advocate, neutral or terrorist) towards you and your competitors. Staying at the personal level, this is also about finding all the negative feelings (anger, shame, sadness and ultimately fear) by which the customer holds themselves back.

- **Client's industry:** where and how does the customer stand in their industry? What are their aspirations? How and where does your customer exceed or fail to meet their customers' expectations? What initiatives are their competitors taking? What political, economic, sociological and technological advances influence them? How do they feel about its/their future?

• **Business:** how does the customer measure success? What level of business knowledge do they want or expect you to demonstrate in: finance, marketing, corporate governance, HR, research and development, manufacturing, logistics and so on.

• **Applying technology:** how does the customer see themselves? As a

- Low cost provider?

- High quality service provider?

and/or

- Advanced technology innovator?

What value does the customer place on the technologies (hardware, software, systems, methodologies, people and know how) you bring to the table?

2. Skills

• **Consultative selling:** is about seeking out truth with customer. Its principles, founded on a basis of trust, go beyond competing to win at any cost. It's about engaging with the client so they can work out the best solution for themselves.

If you feel you have the best value solution for your customer then the only thing that holds them back, from choosing you, is fear. You've won the intellectual reasoning to support your value proposition; what remains is the part where the sale is won or lost. Does the customer see your solution working in their organisation? Does it ring true in their ears? Does it have the right feel? (These are the visual, auditory and kinaesthetic channels through which we reason with ourselves.)

I delved into the process of how to engage a client in a top (consultative) selling fashion in my first article, *Quick Guide - How Top Salespeople Sell.*

• **Coaching and consulting:** by 'consulting', I mean a dialogue where the customer delineates what they know or feel comfortable about, and where/how they will need outside help with the options open to them. The consulting process informs the value that the customer places on outside resources.

Coaching, by contrast, is about helping the customer to develop the willpower, courage, creativity and self-trust to step into the unknown. This is an area I've found that only a handful, the very top salespeople, engage in. Why? Because when you step into the unknown with a customer, you have to trust yourself that the process will arrive at what's best for you both. I've coached salespeople to coach customers with fantastic results. Non-directive coaching requires a different mindset.

It has helped me to explore new ideas and not get hung up if they don't work

Corporate Sales Leader, Top 5 Global IT Company

The majority of salespeople, 'moderates', try to manipulate conversations. They attempt to avoid hidden truths and objections to their cause. Top salespeople live by truth and purposefully seek out all the hidden issues; entrusting themselves and the customer to 'release' them collaboratively.

You cannot release that which you don't know about.

• **Influencing:** is discussed in chapter, *7 Key Traits...*, and covered further in *Quick Guide - How Top Salespeople Sell*

The customer's journey is two parts emotional to one part intellectual. Likewise, the top salesperson engages in a dialogue in the same ratio.

You have two ears to one mouth, the oft used axiom of *spend twice as much time listening with your ears as you speak with your mouth* proves true. Likewise, *spend twice as much time asking questions as answering them* also holds true.

Top salespeople guide customers in and out of problems and opportunities through sensitive and timely questioning that builds the emotional desire to visualise and have the solution proposed. The customer, in effect, persuades themself of what they'd rather have. And will thus be inquisitive as to how the salesperson can make the customer's vision a reality.

• **Negotiating:** I'll add one piece here. When selling to corporations you end up negotiating with 'MAN': the person(s) with the money (or budget), the person(s) with the authority to spend that budget and the person(s) with the need for the solution you propose.

Often these will be three or more different people, each with their own motivations and values they place on your solution. Your objective is to make their value perspectives as resonant and coherent with one another as possible.

Away from the Customer

- **Personal Effectiveness, Account/Territory Management:** optimise the mix of your work to maximise the quality of time spent within the bandwidth available. Top performers spend a higher proportion of their time (compared to 'moderates') performing important/not-urgent (proactive) tasks - as opposed to important/urgent tasks (react mode).

- **Complex Bid Management:** is a process in which top salespeople use the same skills and knowledge that they demonstrate to customers, with their own organisation and business partners. The objective is to ensure that those who are selling the solution have a view of what is being sold that is 100% congruent with those who are delivering the solution. Ultimately this is about engaging the customer so that all stakeholders share the same vision of what is being sold and the value to be achieved.

- **Relationship Strategies with Clients/Internal Networks/External Networks:** as your experience grows you develop the nous to forge successful relationships. As the number of relationships grows and as you start building a reputation, you are then accountable for the image that networks of individuals form of you. Some of these people you will meet infrequently or possibly not at all. The level of collaboration forged across the network emanates in part from the energy you put into it. This is a significant determinant of the success you will have when connecting a network of organisations together to generate complex value propositions. It's also about collaborating to create templates of operation with which people agree to abide by.

I coached a senior salesperson who met a lot of resistance across a network of business partners he was trying to pull together. Eventually he came up with two images:

> *1. A vital cog, at the centre of an engine, trying to control of all the other cogs with the power to say how and when they move*
>
> *2. An intelligent engineer constantly scanning the network, providing fuel and lubricating all its parts to keep the engine running smoothly*

When my client made the switch from the *vital cog* to an *intelligent engineer*, the whole engine kicked into life.

• **Value Generation:** ultimately this is about how you build the map and then plot the route to generate value in the mind and heart of the customer.

Customer value can be assimilated by the following equation:

Value = (what they get + how they get it + additional benefit of doing business specifically with you) / (the cost of doing business with you: directly, indirectly, intellectually, mentally and emotionally)

Essentially, value is the gap a customer perceives between the benefit/cost of doing nothing and doing something. Your task is to engage the customer to paint the picture of the 'bridge' across that gap; make it a real and true reflection of the customer's aspirations. The 'bridge' might need to traverse the customer's innermost fears. Value generation persuades the customer to pick up the paintbrush -and keep a hold of it whilst they paint the most challenging parts of the 'bridge' to reach the other side.

Appendix 2: Three Steps to Be at your Peak in Every Meeting

Write the answers to all the following by hand. Writing as opposed to typing opens up many more neural pathways and thus increases your creativity...

1. Clarify Your Outcomes and the Customer's Outcomes

Ask yourself...

- *What do I want to achieve in terms of...*

    - The task in hand?

    - In terms of my relationship with the customer (e.g. trust, commitment)?

- *What does the customer/person want to achieve or feel in terms of...*

    - Their task in hand?

    - Their relationship with a supplier like me (e.g. reassurance, responsiveness, security, empathy)?

2. Get Yourself in the Right Frame of Mind

Ask yourself...

• *What frame of mind will the other person/people be in when we start the meeting?*

• *What frame do I want them to be in when we finish? (This is your primary objective, to move the customer along the continuum: no interest >> some interest >> interested >> very interested >> energised >> inspired >> convinced >> compelled >> committed.)*

• *What qualities and resources does the customer want me to respect in them? (Keep a 'post it' of your answers in front of you.)*

• *What frame of mind do I want to be in (e.g. focused, composed, objective, friendly)?*

• *What qualities and resources do I want to demonstrate (e.g. attentiveness, sensibility, experience, insightful questioning skills)?*

• *What beliefs (about myself, the customer and the task in hand) will help me achieve the outcomes sought (e.g. 'I am the most helpful to customers with little or no time.' 'This is about me helping the customer to convince themselves.' 'Whether I succeed or not, I will learn from, and be better for, the experience.')?*

3. Prepare in Advance

Ask yourself...

• *What are my motives overall? Who will benefit? Who might not?*

• *What questions would I like to have answers to?*

• *What information do I need/can I get in advance?*

• *What will the other person want to know?*

• *What could I take with me* (facts, data, information, references, visuals, research)?

In the meeting itself...

• Ask for explanation and the reasoning behind ideas/views

• Elucidate ambiguous or 'fuzzy' words

• Explain why you're asking

• Hold a mindset of openness and learning

• Imagine adding each idea to my own proposal

• Imagine being in the other person's shoes (2nd position). Ask self, "Would I advocate this proposal if I was this person? If not, I haven't yet fully understood their position."

• Summarise and feedback to confirm that you've heard the key points correctly

Remember, during the meeting, the most significant (but not the only) factor that will determine a successful outcome (for all) is your *frame of mind.* I'm going to suggest you give this a weighting of 75% in terms of relative importance. Give *clarity about outcomes* a weighting of 20% and having *the right strategy*, 5%. Having all three is important but, during the meeting, it's you who does the selling not the process. People buy from people.

Appendix 3: Sales Managers as Coaches

I've coached, and equipped managers to coach others, who had already been 'trained' in coaching. At the risk of sounding critical (not of people's intentions), here's what I found:

1. Coaching does not particularly have an outstanding reputation in corporate industry. A UK CIPD Learning & Development Survey rated coaching/mentoring as the fourth most effective way of learning, behind on the job learning, formal training and work experience respectively.

2. Grouping coaching with mentoring reveals that, by and large, coaching is misunderstood and misrepresented.

3. Coaching is not mentoring nor is it training. It is a non-directive process to help the client explore and step over the emotional boundaries that they impose on themselves – often unconsciously.

4. Training typically yields a performance improvement of 5-15% at best. Organisations that 'train' managers to coach people thus get results of a similar magnitude to other forms of sales training. They don't achieve the potential they could have achieved by the approach I summarise next.

5. I refer to a coaching approach with which you should be targeting a performance improvement of 30%+.

6. The managers I coached were already equipped with/'trained-in' an oft used coaching technique (*GROW: Goal, Reality, Options and Way forward*) BUT they were not equipped to help their salespeople 'grow' their performance by more than a few percentage

points. Going for, say, 30% growth requires a much more profound approach.

It involves taking people though a structured process outside their comfort zone to do some things very differently, often things that, in the past, they have attached anxiety too. This level of coaching is not a competence that coaches will pick up in a two/three day training course. It requires that they experience passing though their own anxiety barriers – so that they understand more fully the emotional journey that they'll subsequently be coaching others through – by taking their own medicine first.

Here are testimonies from the sales managers I coached, as to what it's like to be coached and subsequently coach people to increase their sales by 30%+. Some refer to specific tools and techniques which they hadn't received in their conventional 'coaching-training'.

Your coaching process gets an A for managing poor performers.*

Using '2nd position' (how to stand in another person's shoes) *has helped enormously. Coaching isn't an individual session; it takes place over a period of time to get to a solution. It's made me face some demons.*

I'm starting to see how powerful this material is.

I took the material and applied it rigorously to coaching X. It's not there yet but the mountain has moved.

I've used the 'Success and Setback Analyses'. (Two tools that 'paint' the boundary by which we engender and limit success.) *I've overcome my shyness... I feel I've moved out of my comfort zone.*

The meeting wasn't easy! I faced my demons and got on with it.

I am more rigorous in the 'Analytical and Process Quadrants' (a 'thinking preferences' analytical tool) *and it's paid off.*

I took away the 'Being at my peak' (see *Appendix 2*) *tool from our session and used it – it's brilliant.*

The 'Being at my peak' (see *Appendix 2*) *tool helps me synchronise with people.*

I am more effective in how I use my time and am more prepared for important meetings.

First two sessions were particularly useful. I would not have got through that month without the self management tool.

When I do follow the coaching process it works and it fails (I fail???) when I don't

...Sales management team members of a Top 5 Global IT Company who, within six months, went on to receive an award for being the top performing sales branch across Europe.

Appendix 4: About me, Paul C Burr

Photo © Stephen Cotterell

I equip people to improve their effectiveness by 30%+ in a matter of weeks, sometimes days.

Business Client: ***"I have worked with Paul periodically over the past 8 years to gain solutions to a number of people issues / opportunities. If you are looking for a Personal Coach to make a High Performer / High performing Team even better (particularly a senior player) – I would not hesitate to recommend him."*** - Sandra Ventre, Management Development Director, Reckitt Benckiser (now with Qantas)

Private Client: ***"You have been so instrumental in the positive changes in my life, I set quite a few goals, and one by one my goals are being achieved, thanks to you, showing me how."*** - Debbie (via Skype) Cape Town, South Africa.

The Skills and Passions in Me

Life doesn't get better by chance; it gets better by change. And change is a journey that's two parts, emotional, to one part, intellectual.

Most of us don't achieve what we set out to achieve at the first attempt. If the outcomes you sought were down to a purely intellectual exercise then you would have achieved them already - would you not? Whether you're a top or moderate performer (or underperforming right now) - every change you make in life is a journey, two parts emotional to one part intellectual. We are twice as likely to hold ourselves back because of self-imposed emotional blocks as opposed to intellectual problems. Put simply, I equip people to tackle challenging emotional journeys.

Corporate clients use me as a 'business coach', personal clients probably see me as more of an 'energy healer'. In both cases I help clients to release the emotional blocks so that they cultivate and apply their innate willpower, imagination, courage and creativity to achieve the business and personal outcomes they seek.

I've over thirty five years of B2B corporate sales and management experience, sixteen years of which overlap with my business and personal coaching work. I've a PhD in Statistics and a First Class Honours Degree in Mathematics. I'm qualified as a Master Practitioner in: NLP, this/past life regression and hypnotherapy.

I give talks (and appear on talk-in shows) on selling, executive coaching, Neuro-Linguistic Programming (NLP), ancient wisdom, football and more ethereal subjects – sometimes to the same audience!

I write books, blogs and am now part way through a series of business articles based upon my own original research, experience and observations in corporate and SME business.

I study and practice ancient wisdom, astrology, casting runes, dowsing, the I Ching and the Tarot.

I love listening to music – rock, jazz, country... you name it. I sing a bit too.

I'm a passionate football fan of Newcastle United Football Club, in "Geordieland", in The North-East of England.

My Promise:

The material I use is powerful, very powerful. I know of nothing quicker or more effective. It's non-mainstream - which means you get non-mainstream results.

The Author in Me

Quick Guide – How Top Salespeople Sell

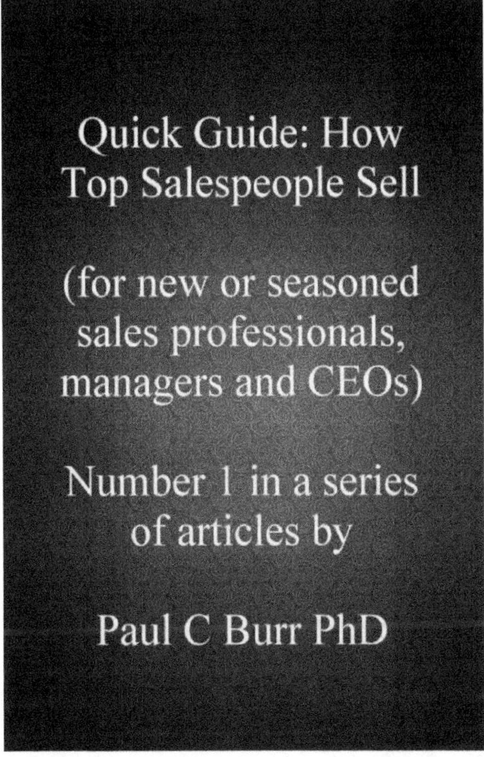

"...a must read for both novice salespeople and the experienced...." - Author, Chiahou Zhang

Learn to Love and Be Loved in Return

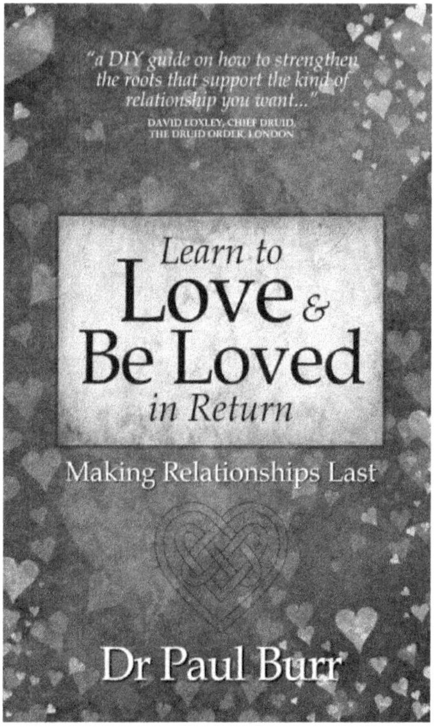

"Uplifting: this is one of those books that arrives in your life at just the right time, when you need it most. The author is able to convey a very deep and meaningful message in an easy to read and understand format with a step by step guide on how to achieve this. The best type of love is unconditional and what better place to start than with yourself." - Rhedd (Amazon reviewer)

2012: a twist in the tail, a novel with spiritual insights

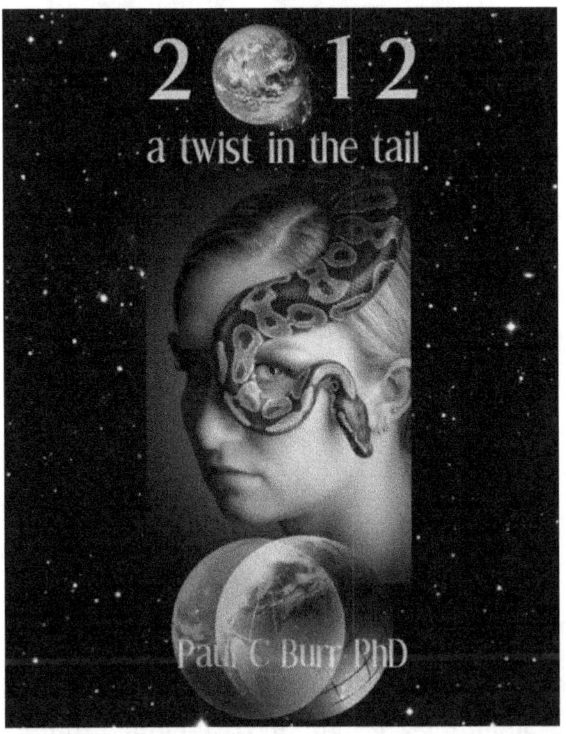

"This is a compelling story for our troubled times. Paul C Burr writes with passion and compassion about moral uncertainties and the quest for salvation and spiritual fulfilment. Go with the flow, trust your inner-self and enjoy this humane and optimistic tale." - Professor John Ditch, York, UK.

"This is a gripping read - beautiful, insightful and very enjoyable. I found phrases and thoughts staying with me, and becoming part of my understanding of the world." - Caroline Eveleigh, *Getting to Excellent*

Defrag your Soul

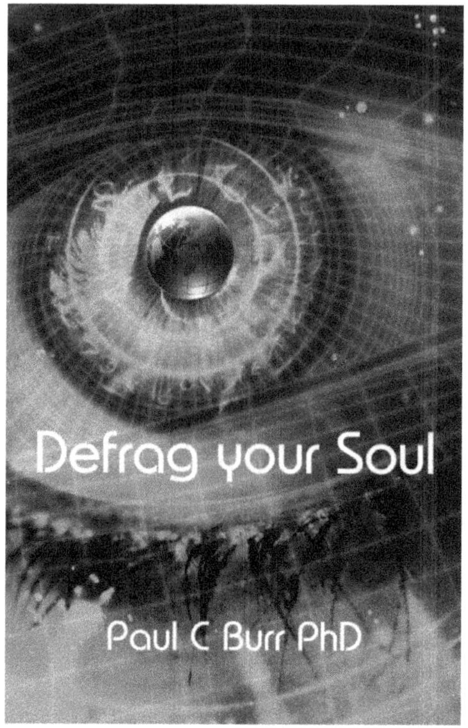

"You should be proud of DYS Paul. I think it is amazing and I'm still thinking hard about what you've written." - Amanda Giles, Author

"DYS whispered to me, 'take heart, be aware, let your journey this far nourish your inner self to be at peace, to love and to shine as your journey continues'." - Penelope Walsh, Book Review

The Blogger in Me

I host a number of Facebook pages that have amassed an aggregate of over 20,000 followers. The most popular page, *Beowulf*, links to extracts from my works as well as the words from others who inspire me.

My blogs cover a broad number of topics to help you in your personal and business life. The 'wisdom' shared comes from what I pick up from day to day life, my research and my client work.

Further Details of Services I Offer over the Internet

You can find out about the quality of the products and services I offer to business and private clients alike, along with a synopsis of my business coaching experience at:

http://paulcburr.com/testimonies/

http://paulcburr.com/private-client-testimonials/

http://paulcburr.com/beowulf_coaching/

The business coaching (and energy healing) sessions work equally well either face to face or over the Internet/telephone services.

For queries, please contact me via *http://paulcburr.com*.

Thank you for your consideration.

/|\

Paul C Burr PhD

www.ingramcontent.com/pod-product-compliance
Lightning Source LLC
Chambersburg PA
CBHW071636170526
45166CB00003B/1334

9781484874615